ISBN 978-618-82970-0-5

Copyright © 2016 & 2020 **Giorgos Kolliopoulos**

Contact: giorgos.kollio@gmail.com
www.speironcompany.com

———

Published by TROPOS Branding Co

5 b, Ioustinianou str. 551 34, Kalamaria
Thessaloniki - Greece
Contact: tropos@tropos.gr
www.tropos.gr

———

NO PART OF THIS BOOK MAY BE PUBLISHED,
SOLD, OR OTHERWISE USED FOR PROFIT
WITHOUT THE WRITTEN PERMISSION OF THE AUTHOR.

———

PHOTO CREDITS
p.34: yoursinglesourcefornews.com / p.35: xdesktopwallpapers.com /
p.36: imperialdesign.pl / p.37: mj777.com / p.38: smirnoff.com /
p.39: kegnbottle.com / p.44: pixabay.com / p.45: wysinfo.com /
p.46: commons.wikimedia.org / p.47: amth.gr, ommons.wikimedia.org /
p.74: sodivin.com / p.75: birkins.cn / p.76: vinchicago.com /
p.88: commons.wikimedia.org / p.89: vertu.com / p.108: commons.wikimedia.org
/ p.109: commons.wikimedia.org / p.110: vacheron-constantin.com /
p.128: pixabay.com / p.129: vimeo.com/jeancharlesrecht

THE FIRST PRACTICAL LUXURY BRANDING GUIDE IN THE WORLD

THE 11 STEPS TO A LUXURY BRAND

Giorgos Kolliopoulos
Creator of λ /lambda/, world's first luxury olive oil

From an entrepreneur that made it happen

Giorgos Kolliopoulos

Entrepreneur, Founder & CEO of Speiron, the first luxury food & beverage company in Greece.

Creator of λ /lambda/ ultra premium olive oil, the first luxury olive oil in the world since 2007.

Giorgos has given a series of motivational speeches and workshops at TEDx, Universities and Luxury Conferences.

Giorgos has also published a series of articles about luxury and luxury branding & marketing. He is considered a luxury branding expert in Greece. He has been awarded for his entrepreneurial achievements from the Chambers of Central Greece.

PREFACE

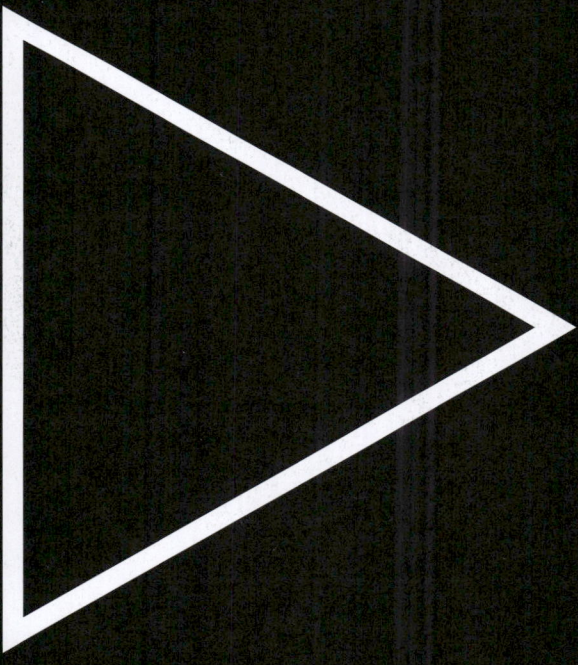

Having re-read and revised The 11 Steps after almost 4 years, I must say that this was definitely an excitement for me:
A journey filled with every success and every failure that I had within the Luxuriant Core. The unique experience that it is deeply hidden inside this ride and waits for you to explore it.

Go out, try, create, succeed and fail as a Luxury Entrepreneur – after all, it is all about a Journey.

Giorgos Kolliopoulos
October 2020

PREFACE

The luxury industry is relatively small in terms of the number of companies. The boundaries are hard to define, but consensus would probably indicate an industry populated by no more than several hundred brands. However these businesses punch far above their weight, both in terms of sales – current estimates put the sale of luxury goods running at more than $100bn per annum – and perhaps more importantly, in terms of influence.

This is the industry where you'll find the best design, the best materials, the best merchandizing and the best packaging, and hence luxury brands frequently lead the way for the rest of the world. In the process they drive both aspiration for the genuine article and the numerous mass-market imitators.

When first discussed with Giorgos Kolliopoulos his idea on publishing his work on Luxury we really said: One more book on Luxury? And in such turbulent times? Then we searched the bibliography and realized that there is no any practical guide on Luxury available. Just a few academic books that need time to read and extract the juice. The decision was made. We would support Giorgos to spread his message to the world by publishing and promoting this remarkable work.

This book comes from an entrepreneur that made it happen. He managed a decade ago to upgrade a commodity food such as olive oil to a Luxury brand renowned now worldwide.

This book is about Extraordinary Vision, Passion for Excellence, Artistic Design, Handcrafting, controlling emotions and creation of the Dream Level, namely the key secrets to decoding luxury.

It will show you how you can apply Extreme Value Added (EVA) to your idea following 11 easy steps and create a unique Luxury Brand that can last for decades.

In this book for the first time new terms and expressions are introduced to the branding world such as AlphaPassion, Always Go Out There In The Dirt, Dilemma Times (DT), ESP Apocalypse, Innovation Fearmeter (IFM), The Mysterious λ, Passion Injection (PI), to name a few.

We know your time is valuable, so our first goal is to present you a book you can read on a brief plane ride. Our second and more important goal is to introduce you the insights, process, and courage to build a successful high-performance luxury brand.

Enjoy!

Christos D. Katsanos & Dimitrios Gartzonikas
January 2017, Thessaloniki

CONTENTS

p.25 / **CHAPTER 1**
What is Luxury

p.61 / **CHAPTER 2**
The Key Secrets of Luxury

p.145 / **CHAPTER 3**
The 11 Steps to a Luxury Brand

p.300 / **A FEW LAST WORDS**

LUXURY

Enigmatic?
Not anymore.

Throughout time

a great number of

luxury companies

emerged + thrived

by offering consumers

unique products

with intriguing passion.

- Belvedere
- Breguet
- Bugatti
- Chanel
- Christian Dior
- Dom Perignon
- Ferrari
- Gucci
- Hennessy
- Hermès
- Jaeger-LeCoultre
- Krug
- Lamborghini

- Louis Vuitton
- Moët & Chandon
- Patek Philippe
- Perini Navi
- Piaget
- Prada
- Rolls Royce
- Tiffany & Co
- Vacheron Constantin
- Vertu
- Veuve Clicquot
- Wally
- Yves Saint Laurent

These iconic companies and many more defined and are still defining what Luxury is truly about.

THIS BOOK IS ABOUT

EXTRAORDINARY VISION,

PASSION FOR EXCELLENCE,

ARTISTIC DESIGN,

HANDCRAFTING,

CONTROLLING EMOTIONS,

THE CREATION

OF THE DREAM-LEVEL.

It will show you
how you can apply
Extreme Value Added (EVA)
to your idea
following 11 easy steps
and create
a unique Luxury Brand
that can last for decades.

The ideas in this book
are applicable
to products mainly.

To **Ian Schrager** & **Mark Divine**

For showing me how to be unique,
how to train mental toughness,
thus how to create change.

> How to read this book

1 / Read front-to-back

2 / Think of your idea

3 / Re-read the headlines or the bold phrases

4 / Re-think your idea, based on what you have read

5 / Begin with execution

6 / Re-read the headlines from time to time to refresh

7 / Be creative, have confidence and trust your vision

8 / Continue with execution

9 / You are there/launch

10 / Always remember that visionaries are scarce, so is luxury and so are you

TERMS & EXPRESSIONS

AlphaPassion	The initial passion you have when you start a business
AlphaPricing	Luxury Pricing, the price tag of a Luxury brand
Always Go Out There In The Dirt	Being present where it happens, in the production process
Brick By Brick Luxury Mission	The procedure of evolving a Luxury business through time
Call To Action	Find your mission, get up and act!
Democratization of Luxury, The	A phenomenon that occurred since the 1950's and resulted in the explosion of Luxury goods' consumption from all social classes
Dilemma Times (DT)	When the going gets tough
Dream-Level	The point where a Luxury brand obtains symbolic value
Elitist Modus	The lifestyle of the Elite
ESP Apocalypse	When your Extraordinary Vision comes to visit you
Extraordinariness Selling Point (ESP)	Your Extraordinary Vision in 6-8 words
Extreme Value Added (EVA)	The symbolic/emotional value of a Luxury brand
Feeling Never Before (FNB)	When you have reinvented yourself and you are feeling that nothing is impossible

Ignorant-Experienced You (IEY)	When you are forgetting what you have been taught in order to innovate
Innovation Fearmeter (IFM)	The measure of fear towards your Mission. Others' fear is usually projected on you, your fear is simply your fear
Low Value Harm (LVH)	A wrong strategic decision or action that can cause harm to your Luxury Vision
Luxuriant Core	The core of Luxury as a phenomenon
LuxuryBorn	Your newly-launched Luxury brand
Luxury Statement	See ESP
Mysterious λ, The	Luxury as an enigmatic Female entity ("Her")
Passion Injection (PI)	When passion runs in your veins instead of blood
Perfectionistic Tendency (PT)	The feeling that perfection should always be reached in all things
Playing Out Of Reach	The Scarcity factor that needs to be built by every Luxury brand
PriceNaut	Your task of setting the right Price for your Luxury Brand
Veblen effect	The more expensive a good, the more increased the demand is

LUXURY

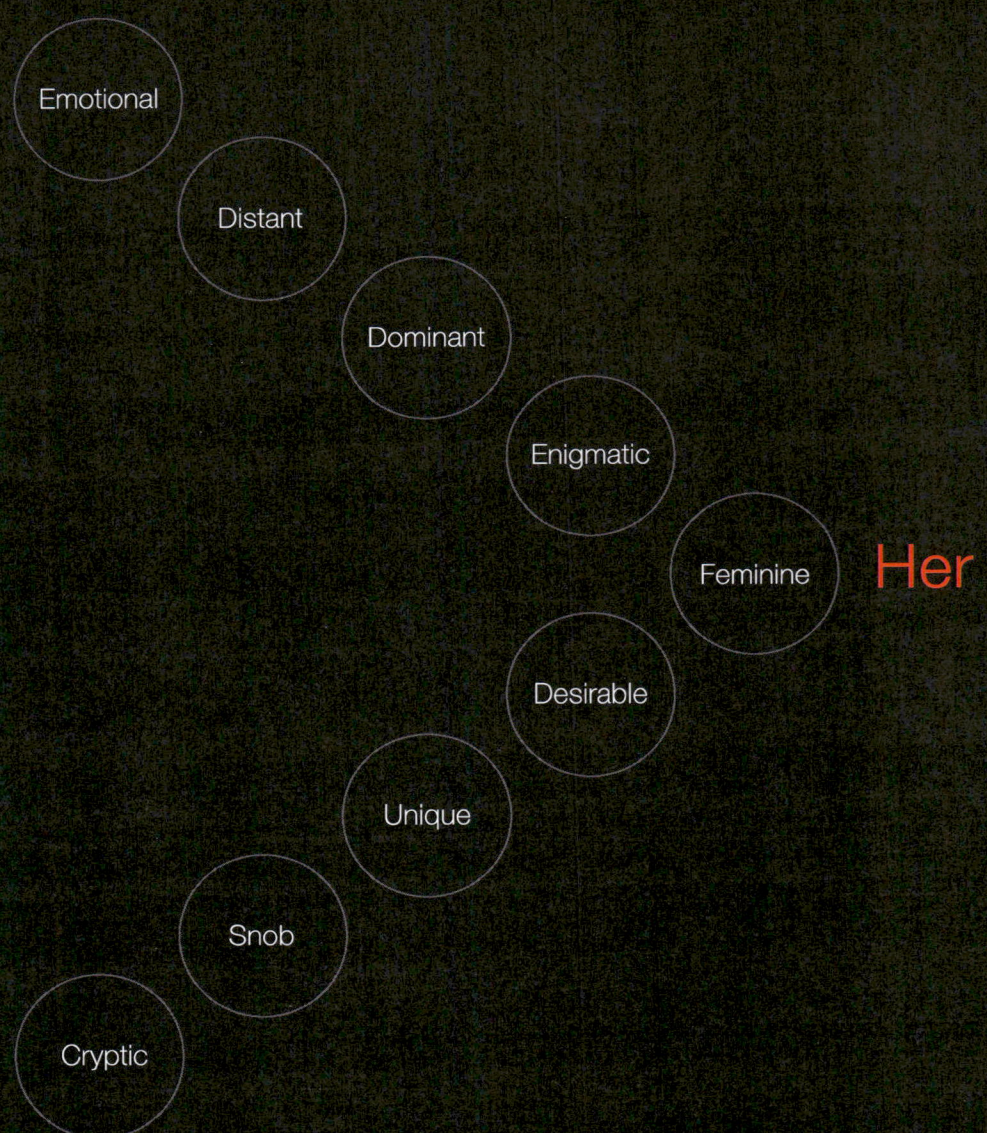

TAKE OFF

CHAPTER 1

What is Luxury

CHAPTER 1

LUXURY ALWAYS ESCAPES US

In order to define
what Luxury is exactly,
we face a number of
difficulties.

It is usually because
Luxury basically constitutes
of EMOTIONS
and not of rational attributes.

We cannot specifically
define an emotion.

But we can definitely
CONTROL an emotion.

I WILL GIVE YOU A FEW DEFINITIONS
OF LUXURY HERE BUT, REMEMBER
LUXURY
is ALL ABOUT
EMOTIONS

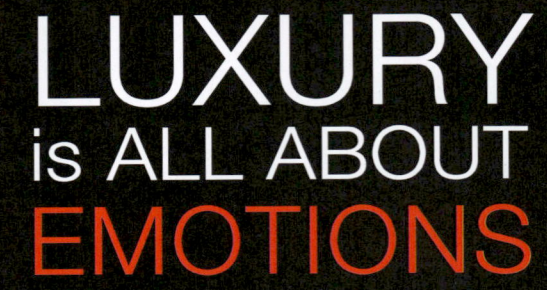

CHAPTER 1

THE MYSTERIOUS ก

Hiding always

There is no real evidence whether
one thing or another
is Luxurious or not.
There is no real argument
as to what is Luxury for me
and what it is for you.

Playing with your emotions

I have to have this supercar
in my garage. My desire
is to own this handbag.
I am in love with this bottle
of champagne. I bought
the shoes of my dreams.

> The next day, I saw
> a new pair of shoes,
> way more expensive
> and started getting
> obsessed with buying
> them too.

Wanting you to want her

Who can say what dreams
are made of?

___

Be it that the unreachable
always attracts us?

___

Are we repeatedly doing
what our desires
are pointing out?

___

Is Mankind a rational or
an irrational being?

___

If we suppose that
we are rational then
why do we keep doing
and buying things
with no reason at all?

CHAPTER 1

LUXURY IS (THE) UNDEFINABLE ?

Before we proceed, we have
to empathize with the idea that there
is no other widely approved definition
for Luxury. So we will use this one:

LUXURY:
Moving from premium to ultra premium

THAT'S IT

Usually, we talk about the
top-of-the-line of a brand,
the most prestigious product
of a certain range.

Their masterpiece,
usually handcrafted,
so unique as to create
enough distance from
all of their other products.

CHAPTER 1

LUXURY
IS WHAT
WE LOVE TO HATE
OR WHAT
WE LOVE TO OWN
BUT
CANNOT
HAVE

Luxury is contradictory, by definition.
We tend to walk away from
luxurious objects and behaviors
while, at the same time,
when a supercar passes by,
we stand still, witnessing
its extraordinary, almost superficial,
design and stare with amazement.

Luxury is almost hypnotic for us:
we strive to avoid her* while we fall in
love with her instantly.

This condition is not be rationalized.
The more you rationalize Luxury
the less you understand human
psychology and its parameters.

---

*Luxury: always her.

CHAPTER 1

LUXURY IS CONTRADICTORY EMOTIONS THAT TURN INTO DESIRES

NOT TO BE CONFUSED!
Premium ~~is NOT~~ Luxury

Premium is, usually, the most
expensive in a typical line of products.

―――――

However it is still one normal product
in a normal (yes, that means boring!)
line of products.

On the other hand, Luxury is a statement.
A luxury product has its own status,
its autonomy. It can "talk" to you,
make you a fan, attract you with its artistic
craftsmanship, extraordinary vision and
superlative pricing.

It's scarce, too. When Scarcity will be further
analyzed, I will explain why being rare is
so important for The Mysterious λ.

CHAPTER 1

EXAMPLE 1

Mercedes C200

- P R E M I U M -

EXAMPLE 1

Mercedes S500

-LUXURY-

CHAPTER 1

--- EXAMPLE 2 ---

iphone

-PREMIUM-

EXAMPLE 2

Vertu

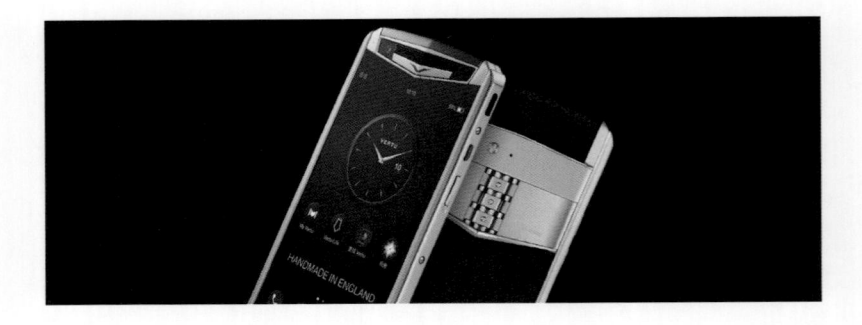

-LUXURY-

CHAPTER 1

EXAMPLE 3

Smirnoff Blue

- P R E M I U M -

40

EXAMPLE 3

Belvedere

-LUXURY-

CHAPTER 1

ALWAYS REMEMBER :

Premium ~~is NOT~~ Luxury

CHAPTER 1

A GLANCE IN HISTORY

Luxury goes back a long way

Death and fear of death will always be mankind's best existential friend.

Luxury was evident in tombs, as proven by the way the ancients buried their dead.

Within those ancient tombs, they placed refined objects, alongside the honored dead such as precious, distinct jewelry or their favorite objects.

All these items clearly showed the social and economic status of the occupant of the tomb.

Surprise.
THIS IS WHEN LUXURY WAS BORN

CHAPTER 1

EXAMPLE 1

Ancient Egypt

The Pharaoh tomb

Refined objects,
buried together with the dead:
The social and economic power
of the occupant of the tomb.

EXAMPLE 1

Ancient Egypt

The invention of glass for storing perfumes

People in Ancient Egypt were the first to discover the use of glass for storing their precious perfumes: Aromatology was born.

CHAPTER 1

EXAMPLE 2

Ancient Greece

The Parthenon

The archetypal temple is highly considered as the temple that set all structural rules. An additional interpretation is needed: arguably, it is clearly a Luxury Statement. The colossal statue of Athena by Phidias, seen as a gold reserve which contained forty talents of pure gold and the many treasures were stored inside the temple (Persian swords, small precious statues) along with the thousands of workers who excavated Pentelic marble 16 km far from the site, all these show an overstatement, the transcendence of Rule (Μέτρον, in Greek).

EXAMPLE 2

Ancient Greece

Pottery & gold vessels

Inspired Greek craftsmen studied
the techniques of creating pottery, bronze,
silver and gold vessels, gem cutting,
ivory carving and jewelry making.

CHAPTER 1

BACK THEN, LUXURY WAS ALL ABOUT THE ELITE

This went on for centuries and centuries. Luxury was being reserved for a very small number of the elite. All others were living an average life, without any real access to culture and its benefits.

It is mostly for that, that Luxury was the inheritor of her own Meritocracy.

Luxury was developed in a truly Elitist Modus over the centuries, that of the rich and famous.

They were the only ones who could participate in The Dream Of The Mysterious λ.

Her name
was LUXURY
but her surname
was ELITE

CHAPTER 1

THEN BOOM

Finally, the second half of the 20th century came

Since then, there has been an ongoing "explosion" in terms of consumption of Luxury Goods.

This was attributed mainly to:
- World Peace
- Women's Rights

These phenomena stimulated the so-called trend of

the democratization of LUXURY

CHAPTER 1

NOW WE CAN ALL PARTICIPATE IN THE LUXURY DREAM

Why did this happen?

———

Was it meant to be?

———

Was Luxury becoming
a boring thing to the Elite?

Of course not. Below are the four milestones for Democratization:

- Luxury goods' spending increase
- Leisure spending increase
- Globalization
- Information Society / Internet

Each and every one of us can be part of the Dream that Luxury has created over centuries for itself. The Elite has now opened its doors to the public. Accordingly, the public is eager to spend time and money on Luxury Goods. Globalization and Information are now as far as a click away. We travel a lot, spend a lot, we would like to enjoy ourselves and have all the info available to do that.

As simple as that.

CHAPTER 1

> REMINDER

LUXURY IS

Undefinable

○

Not to be confused
with premium

○

Moving
from premium
to ultra premium

CHAPTER 1

HOWEVER, THE MOST IMPORTANT THING TO REMEMBER

LUXURY

is contradictory emotions

that turn into desires

———

These

DESIRES

are now

democratically

ours

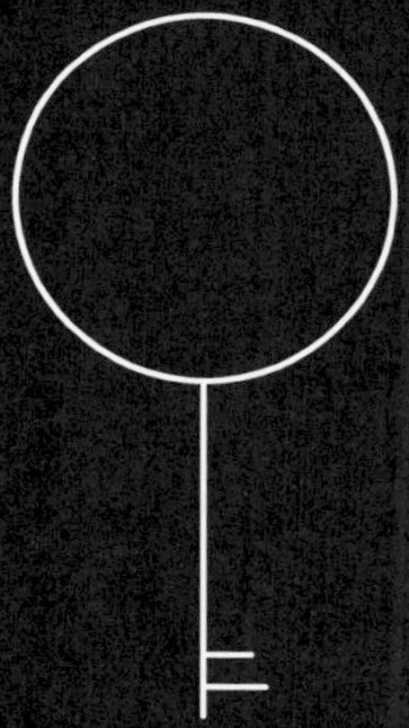

CHAPTER 2

The Key Secrets of Luxury

CHAPTER 2

THE LUXURIANT CORE

Moving into the Luxuriant Core,
we could identify a basic
technique.

She plays constantly with
your emotions. You are either
in or out.

If you are out, it doesn't mean
that you are completely out.
You observe from a distance,
you might be waiting for the
right instance or the right object
of desire.

We all fall for a unique vision
and a stunning execution
and the Mysterious λ
has definitely both.

If you're in, you're totally in.
You will be falling in love over
and over again every time you
meet up with Luxury.

I am always catching myself
admiring a Tourbillon watch,
the mechanism, the looks,
the perfection, everything.
That's it, I'm hooked up.
So are you, all the time,
without even realizing it.

CHAPTER 2

WHAT ARE THE KEY SECRETS FOR DECODING LUXURY

In this chapter,
I will reveal to you
the 4 Key Secrets
that
ALL Luxury Brands
have in common.

This is based on my experience as an entrepreneur and before that as a creative professional who worked in the advertising industry for many years as a copywriter and creative director.

Furthermore, these secrets are based on my brand too, which is a Luxury Brand.

Therefore, this book is based mostly on practice, observation and execution.

CHAPTER 2

LUXURY BRANDS ARE UNAPPROACHABLE, THEY CLEARLY CULTIVATE A MYSTIQUE AROUND THEM

I always wanted
to find out
the **REAL reason**
behind
their mystique.

I came to discover that
somehow I was SUBMISSIVE
to their messages. That surely
means that their messages were
truly to-the-point and
there was authentic
communication between
the Luxury Brand and myself.
Authenticity always works.
It will make you a big fan
so sweetly and gently, that
you won't even notice it.

WHY
DOES THIS HAPPEN?

HOW
DOES THIS HAPPEN?

CHAPTER 2

REMEMBER: LUXURY IS CONTRADICTORY EMOTIONS THAT TURN INTO DESIRES

And there's
a technique to it

Let's see it
through

CHAPTER 2

KEY SECRET

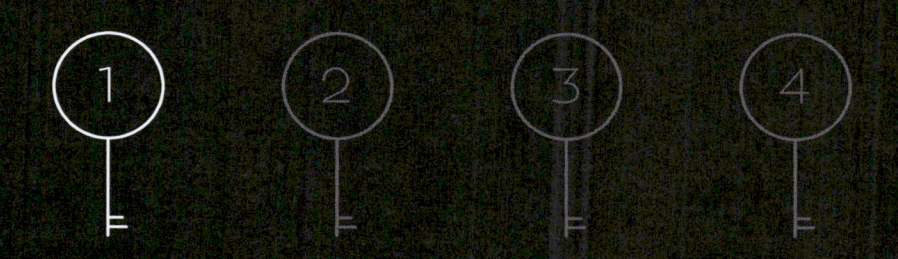

① ② ③ ④
F F F F

HIGH PRICE

CHAPTER 2

WHAT IS THE FIRST THING THAT I SEE IN SOMETHING AND CHARACTERIZE IT AS A LUXURY BRAND?

Average Pricing is
for Average Brands.
In our case, we are talking
about Luxury.

Luxury is the ultimate,
a statement, an extraordinary
set of qualities in one brand.

> Thus, price MUST come
> accordingly. You cannot
> expect people to believe that
> your brand is REALLY unique
> if you set the price low.

Low price is for losers and
the **Mysterious λ**
– make no mistake –
is no loser.

CHAPTER 2

THE PRICE SHOULD ALWAYS BE HIGH, HIGH ENOUGH AS TO CREATE SUFFICIENT DISTANCE FROM ALL OTHERS

Luxury doesn't want proximity

Proximity is unacceptable because it cannot create the aura required for a Luxury Brand.
That's reserved for unique brands only, so

| HIGH PRICE KEEPS NON-ENTHUSIASTS AWAY

Keep it in mind:
High Price is the first and most easily recognizable element of a Luxury Brand.

CHAPTER 2

EXAMPLE 1

Chateau Mouton Rothschild
Jeroboam 1945

Price: €61.000

Note that with a price tag like this,
this is not a wine anymore.
It is a Dream About A Wine or a wine
that is being transformed into a Luxury item.
Thus, the message of the price should be
so strong to keep the non-fans away.

Proximity you said? What's that?
Distance…keep adding distance…always
be remote in order to control emotions
and create tons of desire.

EXAMPLE 2

Hermès
Birkin bag

Price: €250.000

There is no bag in this case.
It is a Dream About A Bag.
Or a bag that is being transformed
into an investment.

Keep raising the price,
keep recreating distance!
That is a basic rule when it comes to Luxury.

CHAPTER 2

EXAMPLE 3

Krug
Grande Cuvée

Price: €265

This is not a champagne anymore.
It is a Dream About A Champagne.
Or a champagne that keeps enough distance
from you and me in order to cultivate proximity
(yes, that's absolutely true according
to the Luxury Universe!).

HIGH PRICING

YOU
vs
THE LUXURY BRAND

CHAPTER 2

YOU
- Makes you want the brand more
- Makes you think it's rare
- Makes you believe it's a privilege to own it

THE LUXURY BRAND
- Raises prices year-by-year in order to take advantage of the Veblen effect: the higher the price, the better Veblen consumers can demonstrate their wealth
- There are no discounts so that we feel it's rare
- There is no direct communication of the price, it is like a best kept secret

YOU

- What you think and desire of a product is its emotional value

- Your perceived prestige and indulgence sets the emotional price

---

THE LUXURY BRAND

- Creates emotional value and sets the emotional price

- Tries not to be considered too snob for your lifestyle, so as to avoid that you'll never become a buyer

CHAPTER 2

KEY SECRET

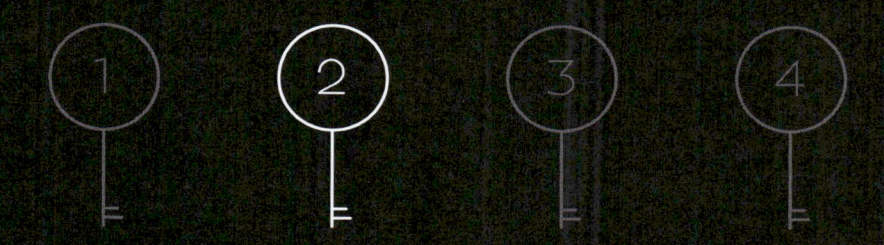

① ② ③ ④

EXTRAORDINARINESS SELLING POINT (ESP)

CHAPTER 2

FORGET
U~~SP'S~~

REMEMBER
ESP'S

Average products have
a Unique Selling Point (USP),
Luxury Brands have
**Extraordinariness Selling
Point (ESP)** instead.

Have you ever wondered
where the mystique of
a Luxury Brand stems from?

> Is it the quality or
> is it the design?
> Is it the status that
> it represents or
> its strive for perfection?

The answer is none of them.

CHAPTER 2

LUXURY BRANDS ARE ALL ABOUT A UNIQUE STORY

The extraordinary vision
of a passionate entrepreneur
that finally came to life

This visionary stood up
and stated something
extraordinary.

So extraordinary that
we are to assume that
all of his/her friends
and relatives could have
never imagined that
this would someday
be brought to life.

This is because the more
unique the vision is,
the less easy it is for people
to understand it.

CHAPTER 2

ESP, THE UNDERLYING PASSION OF ITS CREATOR

The extraordinary
vision
of a passionate
entrepreneur
that finally
came to life

- Be it a stunning creation in the Haute Horlogerie

- Be it a perfectionist's dream about making handcrafted bags

- Be it the vision that one could have about creating an astonishing series of cars that never existed to the day (supercars)

The visionary has a name, has extreme passion and has a specific mission to accomplish. This definitely creates emotional connection with a brand.

CHAPTER 2

EXAMPLE 1

Ferrari

ESP:
The best sports car in the world

Enzo Ferrari was never satisfied with anything.
He was the breed of a perfectionist.
A true visionary, he was curious about finding
original solutions. He founded the Scuderia
at the beginning of the Great Depression:
he was always envisioning the future
rather than staring ecstatically at the past.

EXAMPLE 2

Vertu

ESP:
The most luxurious mobile in the world

Their extraordinary vision was
to market phones explicitly
as fashion accessories,
a concept that was truly unique,
with a stunning ESP:
If you can spend €18.000 on a watch,
why not on a mobile phone?
The first luxury mobile was born.

CHAPTER 2

EXAMPLE 3

λ /lambda/
ultra premium olive oil

ESP:
The first luxury olive oil in the world

I started working on λ /lambda/
in 2006. My ESP was to create
the most stunning olive oil in the world.
One that would be so unique,
so meticulously handcrafted
and so extreme-quality oriented
that would amaze your senses.
The result was a major innovation,
that of the creation of the
first luxury olive oil in the world.

THE PASSION
OF THE VISIONARY

CHAPTER 2

IT CONNECTS YOU EMOTIONALLY AND AESTHETICALLY WITH THE LUXURY BRAND

You feel **connected** with:
- The achievement
- The craftsmanship
- The strive for perfection
- The design
- The cutting edge
- The symbolism that all the above embody

CHAPTER 2

YOUR CONNECTION HAS BEEN CREATING STRONG BONDS WITH THE LUXURY BRAND

YOU ARE FEELING
- Special
- Unique
- Happy
- Loyal

This is why Luxury Brands have so many followers and fans all over the world.

LUXURY BRANDS EMOTIONALLY CONNECT YOU WITH THEIR UNIQUENESS

CHAPTER 2

ESP IS THE HEART OF A LUXURY BRAND

A heart that beats with passion,
gets excited with perfection
and gives life to handcrafted
uniqueness.

You & I will fall many times
in love with this particular heart.

The more
there is passion
into something,
the more we feel
connected

CHAPTER 2

KEY SECRET

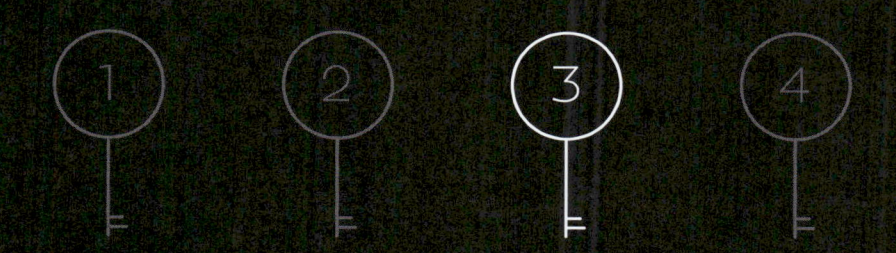

① ② ③ ④

SCARCITY

CHAPTER 2

THIS IS ONE OF THE MOST ESSENTIAL KEY SECRETS OF A LUXURY BRAND

I am going to analyze this
in a while but we shall
keep in mind that:

**ONLY THE SCARCE
IS VALUABLE**

| The more difficult
| it is to find something,
| the more value it creates.

CHAPTER 2

VALUE
ADDED IS DIRECTLY CORRELATED WITH RARITY

WE DESIRE
WHAT WE CANNOT HAVE

We are emotionally
connected to people
and things that are rare
and out of reach

When I feel that something
is of limited supply,
then I begin to desire it.

When I feel that something
is of extremely limited supply,
then I begin to DESPERATELY
desire it.

CHAPTER 2

IT DOESN'T MATTER IF A LUXURY BRAND IS ACTUALLY SCARCE

Emotionally captivated
by the Sirens of Scarcity

In fact, perceived rarity
is all the same to us, as long as
we won't feel that they are
fooling with us.

The emotional desire which
we develop for brands
should be authentic
- at least from our perspective –
and shall be based on
the exclusive relationship
we feel we have with the brand.

Most of the times, it is
a perceived rarity. The more
our radars keep saying that
many people desire this
Luxury Brand because it is
out of reach, the more we want
to emotionally interact with it
in many ways.

CHAPTER 2

HOW IT ACTUALLY WORKS

YOU
VS
THE LUXURY BRAND

THE LUXURY BRAND

- I have to create demand, build scarcity

- The more I am scarce, the more value added I have

- They shall crave for me

YOU

- My friends told me that this new brand produces ONLY 30 items per year. Sourcing of its exclusive materials is demanding. I would very much like to own it!

YOU CANNOT STOP YOUR EMOTIONS FROM DREAMING THE UNREACHABLE

CHAPTER 2

EXAMPLE 1

White Truffle
Tuber Magnatum Pico

Why is it scarce:
Seasonal, not cultivated

White truffles are rare since they are the only truffle variety that cannot be cultivated. They are only available for two months every year. Thus, they are the most expensive on the market and one of the most expensive delicacies in the world.

In 2001, the Tuber Magnatum truffles sold for €4.000/kg. In 2009, they were being sold at €12.800/kg. The record price paid for a single white truffle was set in December 2007, when a truffle weighing 1.5 kg was sold for €300.000.

EXAMPLE 2

Louis Vuitton
Murakami bag

**Why is it scarce:
Limited Edition**

In 2003 American designer Marc Jacobs, who worked for Louis Vuitton, teamed up with Japanese designer Takashi Murakami and created a limited edition known as "Cherry Blossom" bags. This edition was quickly sold out. In addition it caused long waiting lists all over the world. The profits were over 250 million euros in 2003 alone. This series was and still is one of the most sought-after line of bags in the history of fashion.

EXAMPLE 3

Vacheron Constantin
Ref. 57260

Why is it scarce:
Only one piece

Launched in 2015, Vacheron Constantin's Ref. 57260 it is the most complicated mechanical pocket watch in the world. This watch features 57 complications. It took eight years to assemble, has 2826 parts and 31 hands and it weighs 957 grams.

The estimated price paid from its sole owner was over €10.000.000.

A FEW ISSUES TO DEAL WITH

THE LUXURY BRAND
VS
YOU

CHAPTER 2

THE LUXURY BRAND

- Needs to keep up with exclusivity and scarcity
- Wants to expand and increase sales

YOU

- Need to feel that this always remains out of your reach, otherwise you will not pay for it

---

LUXURY BRANDS
HAVE TO PRETEND
SO THAT YOU WILL
STAY EMOTIONALLY
CONNECTED

PLAYING OUT OF REACH

THE LUXURY BRAND
vs
YOU

CHAPTER 2

THE LUXURY BRAND

- Will communicate that it is a limited edition, even if it is not
- Will place itself in very selected outlets
- Will communicate its launch through word-of-mouth channels
- Will publicize the names of celebrities that are customers through word-of-mouth channels
- Won't communicate the price directly, as it violates the snob effect
- Will continuously "play out of reach", checking every now and then that everything is ok (read Snob)

YOU

- Just heard it: this is the most expensive (you name it) in the world
- Let me check the price
- Ohhhh....why is it so expensive?
- Is it worth the price?
- They say that they only make 2.000 of them each year
- Ah, now I just saw that they sell it at (name the place)
- I heard that Madonna uses it regularly
- Do you think that it will be a good idea if I would buy their entry level brand, which stills looks cheap to me (but IT'S NOT!)?

CHAPTER 2

EVERY TIME A LUXURY BRAND COMMUNICATES A LAUNCH:

You shall look for

- Associations of *scarcity*
- Limitations in production
- Difficulties in sourcing
- Seasonalities
- Third parties and not direct communication (PR, bloggers etc.)
- Top level placements
- Celebrity endorsements
- Exclusive events

CHAPTER 2

WE CANNOT HAVE LUXURY WITHOUT SCARCITY

Scarcity is the
"something-that-is-missed".

This is what makes it
so intriguing.

We are usually in a condition
of mixed emotions when it comes
to intrigue and mystery.
We expect reactions of
attachment and intimacy,
an irrational desire that controls
our emotions, thus influences
our reactions.

Therefore, if we are to understand
why we react so intensely
to Luxury it is mainly because
that's the missing piece.

> AND THAT PIECE
> SHOULD NEVER EVER
> BE PUT IN ITS PLACE
> IN ORDER TO COMPLETE
> THE IMAGINED PUZZLE

CHAPTER 2

TO CONCLUDE
ABOUT SCARCITY

- It is the most powerful of all the tools that the Mysterious λ uses

- It is EMOTIONAL

- It is there to dominate your emotions, to control them

- When you open your door to Scarcity, you recognize value added to a Luxury Brand

- When you refuse to close the door to Scarcity, you continue to see value added to a Luxury Brand

- When you close the door to Scarcity, this brand is not Luxury (for you) anymore

CHAPTER 2

KEY SECRET

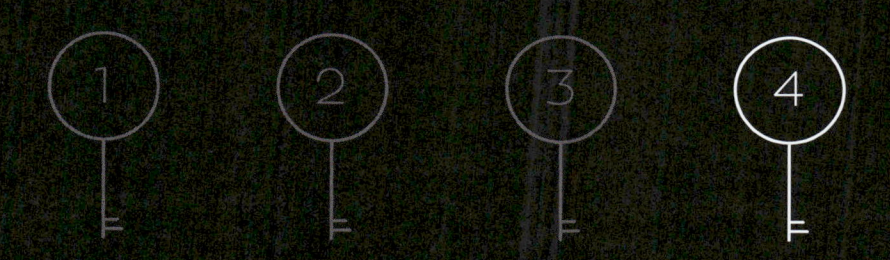

① ② ③ ④

CRAFTSMANSHIP

CHAPTER 2

PERFECTIONISM AS A SYMBOLICAL VALUE

Now let's examine
the fourth and last element
in a Luxury Brand,
that of craftsmanship.

With that being said, I mean
the SYMBOLIC interpretation
that craftsmanship has in
the Luxury Universe.

CHAPTER 2

ARTISTIC DESIGN

Sophisticated design always
characterized Luxury Brands.
It goes without saying that Luxury,
as a statement, embodies
the Art Of The Human Hand

———

A true Luxury Brand
is an extraordinary Strive
for Perfection.

Don't they say that Perfection
lies in the Details?

THE LUXURY BRAND

- Builds on heritage
- Achieves extraordinary design
- Strives for perfection
- Speaks out its craft skills
- Shows craftsmanship at work
- Names the exact hours, months and years that it took for the creation
- Brings the craftsman together with customers at special events

CHAPTER 2

EXAMPLE 1

Rolls Royce

Bespoke Team

When you commission a Rolls-Royce,
their Bespoke team collaborates with you
in order to fulfill your every wish. They use detailed
drawings, computer-generated blueprints
and master craftsmanship in order to bring
your unique request to life. In their website, they
feature a series of Bespoke cars and their stories as
well as extensive photos of craft skills.

EXAMPLE 2

Dom Pérignon

The restoration of Abbey Saint-Pierre

In 2009, Dom Pérignon commissioned the restoration of Abbey Saint-Pierre in Hautvillers. They used master craftsmen and local materials for the work. After more than eighteen months of research and preparation work, it took two craftsmen from the Compagnons du Devoir organization three months to renovate. They had used materials made out of oak from the Ardennes Forest and specially-made tools to reproduce the original moldings.

CHAPTER 2

EXAMPLE 3

Salvatore Ferragamo

Salvatore Ferragamo

The Art of Shoemaking 2015

In July 2015, Salvatore Ferragamo,
one of the best shoemakers in the world,
held a live showcase of a master craftsman at work.
It demonstrated the process behind the making of
their hand-made shoes along with the superior-quality
materials used. This occasion was open to the public and
took place outside the Salvatore Ferragamo store
in Pavilion, KL.

LUXURY AS AN EXPERIENCE

THE LUXURY BRAND
VS
YOU

CHAPTER 2

Let's see how
the Luxury element
affects our emotions

YOU

- Feel associated with the brand
- Want to know more about their history
- Want to be a part of it
- Share stories that spread word-of-mouth
- Experience the brand rather than own it

YOU WANT TO INDULGE YOURSELF?

Here's an object of desire!

CHAPTER 2

21ST CENTURY LUXURY

Luxury Brands would introduce unique experiential environments so that we could feel precious and special when purchasing them.

This is exactly why Craftsmanship proves to be a very important tool for the **Mysterious λ**.

The human aspect, the artisan, the perfect skill, the artistic element, the stunning design: Desire, passion, excitement, perfection, attention to the smallest detail.

Luxury gives us
more than one reason
to surrender
to an ocean of emotions

CHAPTER 2

EVERY TIME YOU LOOK AT A PHOTO OF A LUXURY CRAFTSMAN:

What to notice

- Assume that it is definitely a strategy

- It shows that Luxury and Mastery Skills are historically tied together

- Assume that all artistic influences are prerequisites for a Luxury Brand

- Be assured that they very much want YOUR connection

CHAPTER 2

LUXURY AND THE CULTURE OF EXCELLENCE

THE LUXURY BRAND

- Strives for perfection
- Is obsessed with quality
- Establishes expertise
- Has deep cultural roots
- Aims to control production at a highest level
- Epitomizes handcrafting
- Stands as an achievement of human art and passion

CHAPTER 2

\\

I am not buying
the object itself.

I am connecting with
the excellence, the devotion
and the timelessness
behind the object.

I am enthralled by the story,
the passion and the commitment that
brought it to life.

//

TO CONCLUDE

- Craftsmanship embodies Luxury's emotional and rational aspects. Without the human skill, we cannot identify ourselves with the extraordinary vision

- The meticulous attention to detail will always be timeless

- The **Mysterious** is nothing but ephemeral

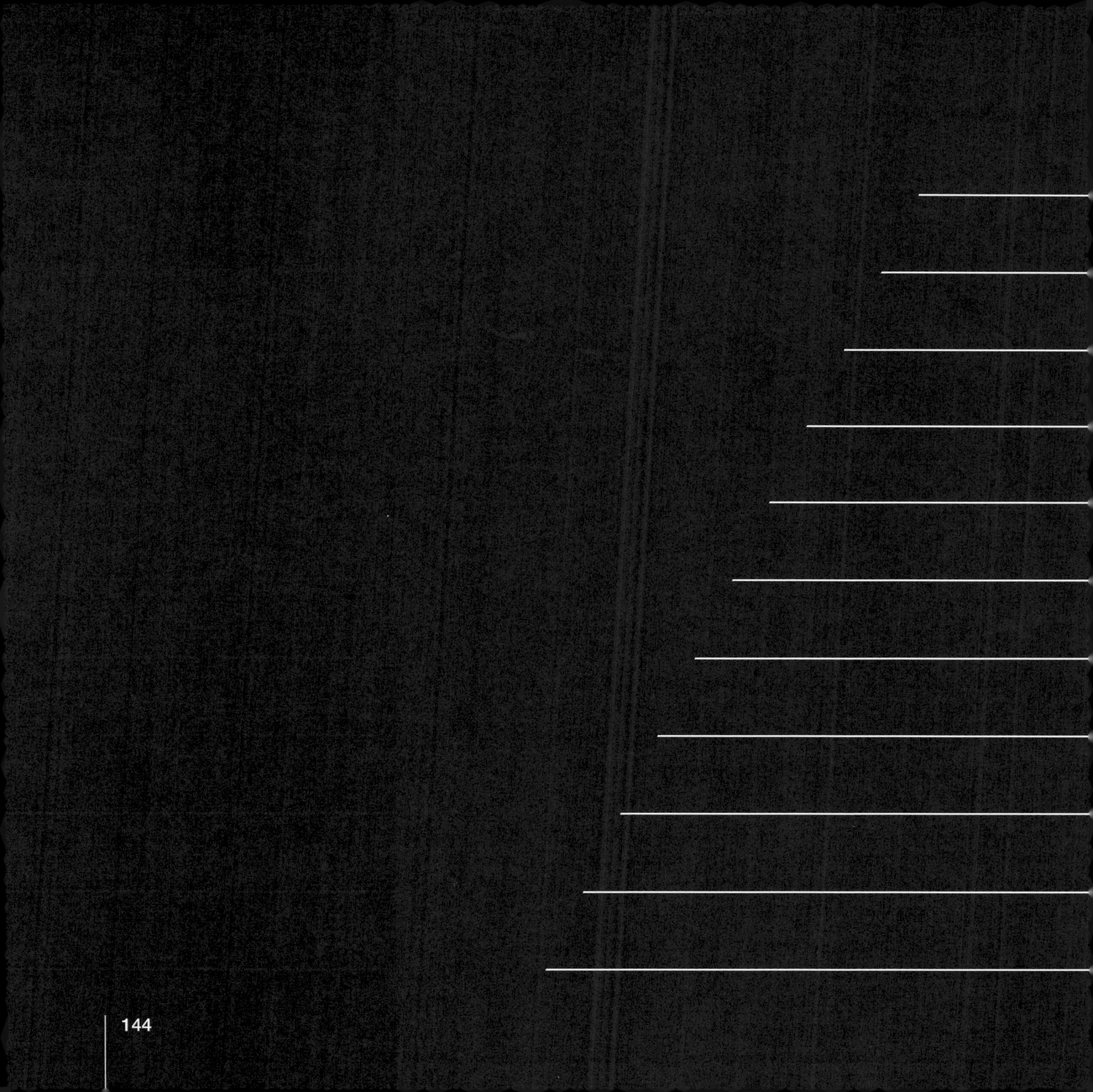

CHAPTER 3

The 11 Steps to a Luxury Brand

CHAPTER 3

HOW TO ADD EXTREME VALUE ADDED (EVA) TO YOUR BRAND

Now we get to the real point
of this book.

I have been an entrepreneur
since 2006.

I launched a luxury brand that
simultaneously became a major
innovation in its sector.

> I observed and
> practiced and failed
> in many things during
> all these years and
> I want to share them
> with you.

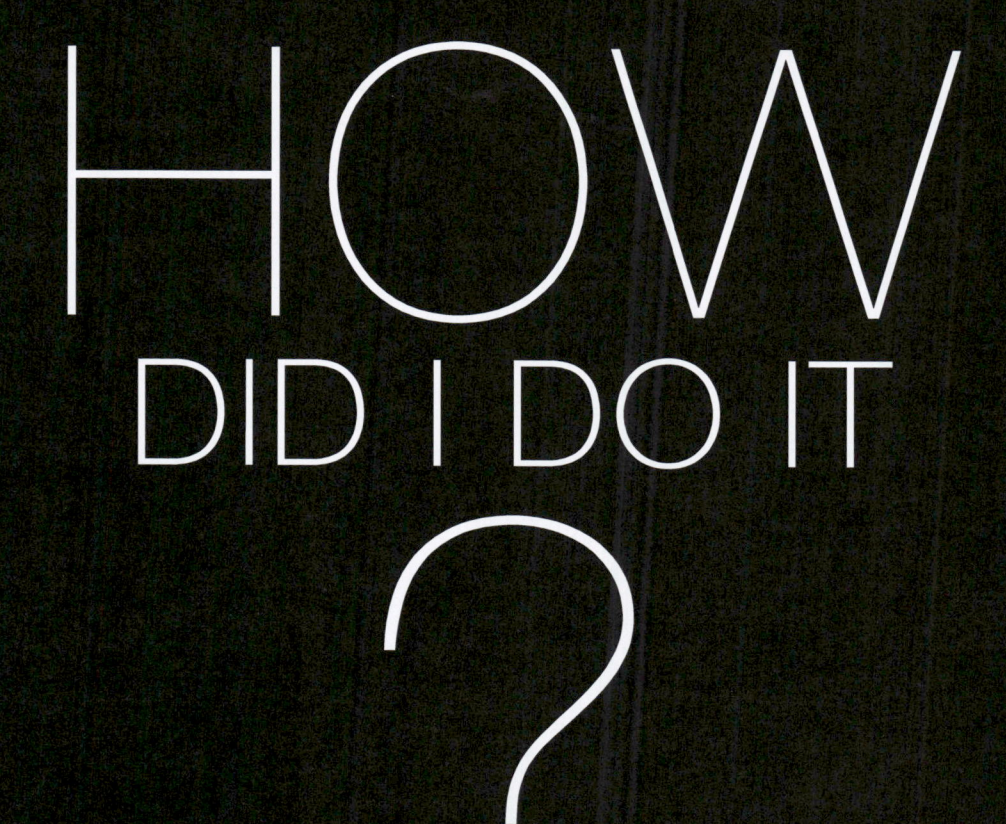

CHAPTER 3

HOW
DID I DO IT
?

First I never looked back.
Once I realized what I wanted to do –
and that was a transcendence
of Μέτρον (Greek for Rule) thus
a Luxury Statement – I begun to find
my ESP.

My passion was always there,
my perfectionism never left me
and the only thing that had been
missing at that point was
EXECUTION.

This is a book
about execution,
real life, not just ideas
and theories
of a professor.

Entrepreneurs
know better
because their actions
speak always louder
than their words.

CHAPTER 3

READY? HERE WE GO...

THE 11 STEPS TO A LUXURY BRAND

STEP 1
Fail Student

STEP 2
Innovator Mania

STEP 3
Innovation Gap

STEP 4
ESP Apocalypse

STEP 5
Momentum Blast

STEP 6
Luxury Baby

STEP 7
Luxury Adolescent

STEP 8
Luxury College Student

STEP 9
Luxury Adult

STEP 10
Luxury Adult + Kicking

STEP 11
Luxury Adult + 2X Kicking

CHAPTER 3

STEP 1

FAIL STUDENT

CHAPTER 3

YOU HAVE TO HAVE FAILED BEFORE ATTEMPTING A LUXURY VENTURE

All entrepreneurs have failed more than once. Failure is the most VALUABLE lesson in life.

I was fired from two companies in a row and within a year, before attempting to be an entrepreneur.

I got depressed. It's normal, that's the way it is. Accept it.

It took me far more time then to accept failure than it would have taken me now.

CHAPTER 3

ACCEPT
FAILURE AND LEARN FROM IT

I began to analyze why I was down. I realized that it was not something personal. It was the way that things are. Sometimes, you cannot change things.

So, I got up. Day by day, month to month.

I started to see the world around me from a different perspective.

THAT'S WHAT FAILURE DOES
IT GETS YOU TO ZERO
SO THAT YOU CAN START
BUILDING AGAIN.

CHAPTER 3

WHEN YOU FAIL, FAIL FAST

I see now that, back then,
I was slower in getting up
and trying again.

———

There was a reason for that:
**I HADN'T FAILED
SO MANY TIMES**

Experience in failure
is experience in getting up
real fast.

Therefore, learn to fail as
many times as possible
in order to get up and go on
with a new venture.

**FAILURE IS YOUR ENEMY
AT FIRST
AND YOUR MOST VALUABLE
ALLY IN THE END**

CHAPTER 3

BE A FAIL STUDENT

- Fail before

- Fail as much as possible

- Learn to fail on purpose

- Accept failure

- When you are feeling down,
  try to analyze and not paralyze

- Learn to fail fast

- Visualize your way up

- Start elevation

- When you are feeling up,
  visualize failure and expect it
  to happen many times again
  in the future

THAT'S IT
YOU ARE NOW A FAIL STUDENT,
READY FOR ACTION.

CHAPTER 3

STEP 2

INNOVATOR MANIA

CHAPTER 3

WHAT'S THE THING YOU ARE MOSTLY IN LOVE WITH?

I am in a passionate, romantic
LONG TERM relationship with
coffee and olive oil. I am totally
in love with both of them.

When I begun seeking THE IDEA,
I wasn't exactly aware that
the idea was IN FRONT OF ME.

It would be either coffee
or olive oil.

**LOOK FOR
A SPECIFIC PASSION
THAT'S INSIDE YOU**

CHAPTER 3

IDENTIFY
YOUR PASSION

It will be you who will know
that THIS IDEA is your passion
and it is better than THAT IDEA.
Only you and nobody else, because
if the passion is not yours and it is
implemented by somebody else, IT
WILL CERTAINLY FAIL.

Remember, coffee and olive oil
were my main motivators. The
things that I was passionate for.

Your passion should be headed
into achieving YOUR specific
goals and not that of others.

**YOUR PASSION
ALWAYS HAS A NAME,
YOUR NAME**

CHAPTER 3

PASSIONATE
+
KICKING

The essential thing
about passion is that
it gets you moving.

———

Passion is by far the most important psychological element so that you can feel you CAN ACTUALLY do it.

WHEN YOU ARE IN PASSION INJECTION (PI) MODE

- You wake up every morning to do extraordinary work

- You feel your blood rushing into one direction

- You have a force of 1.000 HP pushing you forward

- You accept fear, for this you can control it really quick

- You are your own motivator

- You can motivate other people to join in as well

CHAPTER 3

WHEN IN PASSION, ALWAYS IN
PASSION

When I was starting
my business, I felt that
something was happening
inside me: I was Feeling like
Never Before (FNB).

It was so strong and powerful
and alerting that it has been
keeping me alive for many years,
passionate, always reaching for
my possible and impossible best.

Passion keeps you cool in your
days of difficulty and unaffected
in your days of easiness.

**IN DILEMMA TIMES (DT),
UNLEASH YOUR DRIVING
FORCE**

CHAPTER 3

THE JOURNEY
IS THE MISSION

All entrepreneurs
share something
in common: they are
in love with the journey, not
the destination.

Most people prefer the destination, the end of it. So they always ask about how much time this will take to succeed, how many years it will take to make you a millionaire and so on.

This is boring. I know from my personal experience that if it wasn't for my passion to be different, I wouldn't have done it.

**ENJOY THE RIDE,
THE UPS AND DOWNS,
USE YOUR CREATIVITY
AND SMILE**

CHAPTER 3

STEP 3

INNOVATION GAP

CHAPTER 3

IS THERE SOMETHING
MISSING

?

Now you know how it is
to fail and you are passionate
with your vision to succeed.
There's something missing,
though.

And that's to identify
an innovation gap.

The one piece that is missing
from a sector. The one
experience that no one has
claimed up-to-now.

**INNOVATION LIES
SOMEWHERE BETWEEN YOUR
PASSION AND A MARKET GAP**

CHAPTER 3

HOW
CAN YOU DO IT?

- You look for something that you love

- You read exhaustively for days and months so as to know as many things as possible about it

- You gain some special knowledge (attending courses, conferences, etc.)

- You are becoming more competent now

CHAPTER 3

FORGET
YOUR
EXPERTISE

When I started, I was in love with coffee and olive oil as I stated earlier. So these two things were to be explored by me as possible business ventures.

Coffee didn't make it to the end. I will explain why a little bit later. And so I was left alone with the olive oil and my passion for it.

I was curious to read as much as possible on this subject. I was the perfect student. My passion and Perfectionistic Tendency (PT) drove me to take a course on how to assess olive oil's exceptional quality. The whole procedure took me 3 months.

WHEN YOU THINK YOU'VE LEARNED IT ALL...

CHAPTER 3

THEN YOU KNOW THAT YOU SHOULD IMMEDIATELY FORGET ALL THAT YOU HAVE JUST LEARNED

Many people would talk about
innovation. They suggest that
innovation occurs when
you invent or reinvent something.

I will not argue with that.

But in this chapter, I would like
to explore what you might be feeling
BEFORE you innovate.

| **WHAT WOULD YOU FEEL BEFORE ATTEMPTING TO FIND THE MISSING PIECE?**

CHAPTER 3

THE
FIELD-TESTED
ROUTE
TO
INNOVATION

FORGET
all that
you've learned

That's it. Just forget it all. Be a Tabula Rasa again. It doesn't matter what they teach you or what you learned or how good of a student you were in the first place. It doesn't matter how many hours or days or months you spent wanting to be the best in it.

THE ONLY THING
THAT MATTERS NOW
IS TO
**FORGET YOUR EXPERIENCE
NOW YOU HAVE IT**

CHAPTER 3

THE INNOVATION GAP (IG) REVEALS ITSELF

Experts usually don't know anything about an innovation. They just don't want to get out of their box of knowledge. Because they simply FEAR innovation.

The IG is for you and me. And you will notice the Gap as soon as you discover the Ignorant-Experienced You (IEY).

Let's play the game of conscious ignorance in order to see the subject from "above" and identify the missing piece. This is what I did with the olive oil. I saw it like that and identified the innovation of a luxury olive oil.

> **THE MORE YOU PLAY WITH IGNORANCE, THE LESS FEAR YOU HAVE**

CHAPTER 3

STEP 4

ESP APOCALYPSE

CHAPTER 3

THE FIRST KNOCK KNOCK OF THE Mysterious λ

You have
identified the IG.

———

You know
what to do.

———

You just found
your Mission.

The Mission is closely related
to your Passion.

When I found out that
my missing piece was
"an ultra premiumization"
of the olive oil, I got so excited
that I couldn't sleep normally
for days.

I was thinking about my ESP.

**ESP LEADS YOUR
EXTRAORDINARY JOURNEY
TO EXECUTION**

CHAPTER 3

APPLYING KEY SECRET
ESP

When your **apocalypse**
will knock the door,
you will definitely know it.

———

It may come as a dream.

It may come through
brainstorming.

It may come when you walk
in the woods or when you swim
in the sea or the pool.

It may come as a surprise.
But surprise it is NOT.

This was the reason why I didn't
venture into the coffee business.
Because coffee was much more
exploited by others, thus no
apocalypse for me there.

> **THE MISSION
> WILL BE IN TOUCH
> IF YOU FOLLOW
> THE RIGHT STEPS**

CHAPTER 3

100%
MISSION
IN 6-8 WORDS

In order to complete
THE FIRST PHASE
of your Mission,
you need to express it.

Just like your favorite song,
the words will automatically
come to your brain, as a mantra.

My ESP was to create "the most
stunning olive oil in the world".
Of course it was a Luxury Claim,
as it was way above average and
way above premium.

**As you remember,
premium is NOT Luxury.**

**YOUR INNOVATION MANTRA.
YOUR ESP**

CHAPTER 3

IGNORE FEAR, ALWAYS GUARD YOUR ESP

Ignoring others, especially
if they are very close to you,
can be difficult. But you should
guard your ESP no matter what.
It is your precious Mission and
NO ONE will have a say on that.

REPEAT : NO ONE

Ignore fear of others, control your
fear, concentrate totally on your
Mission towards the Mysterious λ.

> ALWAYS VISUALIZE
> YOUR **ESP**,
> IT WILL HELP YOU
> DOWN THE ROAD

CHAPTER 3

STEP 5

MOMENTUM BLAST

CHAPTER 3

THE WINDMILLS OF YOUR MIND

This is the time when
you will begin to see things
more clearly.

―――――

When you started, it was probably
some kind of a mess.

You didn't exactly know what
you were going to do. You knew
what drove your passion but you
didn't understand what to do with it.
You read a lot of things about
the subject, even got some
specialization on the topic,
but again there was something
missing.

CHAPTER 3

THE ESP
APOCALYPSE

Then came
the ESP Apocalypse
and the fear of others
(maybe yours, too)
kicked in.

Your passion and determination
helped to avoid an extreme
increase of fear.

THEN?
WHAT IS THE NEXT STEP?

CHAPTER 3

ENJOY YOUR MOMENTUM BLAST

Momentum is not about
you or your venture.

———

Momentum is about
you AND your venture.

**WHEN THE TIME IS RIGHT,
YOU WILL SURELY KNOW IT**

CHAPTER 3

CREATIVE EXPLOSION

My experience tells me that when momentum kicks in, you need to *explode*.

For what is entrepreneurship but an explosion of creative energy?

YOU

- Have the knowledge
- Forgot the knowledge
- Have the passion
- Found your ESP
- Are brain stimulated
- Avoid and control fear
- Are invincible

CHAPTER 3

THIS IS THE TIME.
AS ALWAYS,
THE TIME IS
NOW

Luxury is this Finest Execution
to the Smallest Detail.

———

You feel confident and you know the way.
You have what it takes to.

**EXECUTE LIKE YOU ARE
THE BEST IN THE WORLD**

CHAPTER 3

STEP 6

LUXURY BABY

CHAPTER 3

3·2·1
EXECUTION TIME!

How you can do it

REMEMBER

You have to apply ALL 3 Key Secrets (you have already found your ESP) in order for your Luxury Brand to be born.

Have you chosen your raw material and are you now thinking what your next move is? It's as easy as re-reading this book.

CHAPTER 3

WHEN IN ESP MODE
EXPLODE

You should express it
in words and write it down.

———

You should share it
with other people.

CHAPTER 3

INNOVATION FEARMETER

Expect FEAR projected from them
to you. When there is no fear from others
directed to you, there is no innovation.
Simple as that.

The more innovative your ESP is,
the more fear you should expect.

**It's called
the Innovation Fearmeter
(IFM).**

> **THE ONLY WAY FOR THE
> IFM NOT TO DRASTICALLY
> INCREASE, IS FOR YOU
> TO EXPLODE CREATIVELY**

CHAPTER 3

APPLYING KEY SECRET
CRAFTSMANSHIP

Surrender to Craftsmanship

You have to let go of creating something ordinary, cheap looking, "me-too" designed and definitely boring.

This is NOT what this book was written for.

Everything precious around you calls for extraordinary design, craftsmanship and passion for excellence.

YOU NEED TO THINK OUTSIDE OF THE BOX AND

> **FORGET** EVERYTHING YOU KNOW ABOUT PACKAGING

CHAPTER 3

YOUR PACKAGING WON'T SEEK
PRETENTION

It shall include
- A shape like no other
- Eye-catching factors
- 80% craftsmanship - 20% industrial elements
- Dogmatic branding

These are all indispensable because your consumer wants NOTHING common.

**CREATE TO STAND OUT
NOT TO STAND STILL**

CHAPTER 3

IN ORDER TO CREATE YOUR LUXURY BRAND

You have to do the completely opposite of what the sector does

THE "COMPETITOR"

Sells their brand in a plastic packaging. That's what all "competitors" are doing in the moment

---

YOU

You HAVE to invest in handcrafting, hire a craftsman and create a totally unique handcrafted packaging

THE "COMPETITOR"

The "competitor" is selling their brand as a high quality vodka. That's what all "competitors" are doing at the moment

---

YOU

You HAVE to build on emotions and uniqueness; thus, you have to be selling THE DREAM of a Luxury Vodka

CHAPTER 3

DON'T YOU DARE NOT TO LOOK AT ME!

**If you succeed
in getting this reaction
from any customer,
congrats,
you are now
in the Luxury Zone**

By placing the raw material in unprecedented packaging, you have the impression of excellence covered.

Then, it's the feeling of the materials used. By simply touching the brand, one should feel precious, elect, honorary welcomed.

This is what craftsmanship would achieve. The feeling has to be incomparable for this sector.

Finally, the logo shall have eye-catching elements which make it unforgettable, dogmatic: once seen, never forgotten.

CHAPTER 3

THE
VIEW MASTER
OF
EMOTIONS

**Your Luxury Baby
is now alive + kicking**

You have successfully completed
the execution phase.

You have completely ignored
what the competition does
in order to create a Baby
that's kicking differently than
any other baby.

CHAPTER 3

They stand for
Me Too
≠
You stand
for Unique

They stand for
Mass Production Line
≠
You stand for
Craftsmanship

They stand for
Cheap Materials
≠
You stand for
Finest Fabrics

They stand for
products

≠

You stand for
FEELINGS & DESIRES

CHAPTER 3

STEP 7

LUXURY ADOLESCENT

CHAPTER 3

EMOTION CONTROLLER?
YES YOU CAN

Now that you have your LuxuryBorn in front of you

You would need to play more and more with emotions, to control dreams and evoke desires.

High pricing is your ally, as it transmits subconsciously the right message.

IGNORE COMMON PRICING

CHAPTER 3

APPLYING KEY SECRET
HIGH PRICE

Forget the Baby, welcome the Valued Adolescent!

Do a research about your competitors and their pricing strategies and then "forget" everything about this research.

Begin to value YOUR brand rather than theirs. Stay focused on your perspective about this extraordinary mission.

> **PRICE IS THE VALUE YOU HAVE INCLUDED INTO YOUR CREATION**

CHAPTER 3

A BATH IN
VALUE
ADDED ++
EMOTIONS

There isn't really any competition
in the Luxury Universe. There are
only vague emotions that turn
into desires.

The more persuasive you are
in doing that, the more
Value-Added Space
you have created.

Therefore my brand WAS NOT
to be compared to other Luxury
Brands.

λ /lambda/ was to stand out
as A STATEMENT of my passion
and vision.

**EUROS? DOLLARS?
NO. IT'S YOUR PASSION
THAT PROVOKES
CONNECTION**

CHAPTER 3

THERE'S NO STRATEGY IN LUXURY
PRICING

Assuming that the average price
of most competitors is €10,
if you are to place your price
at €100 or €1.000, do you think
that is there really a difference
for your customer?

Your price should be distant
from any competition. You are
passionate and perfectionist,
therefore Snob!

You have just created the best
(you name it) in the world.
You aren't playing THEIR game.
You are the master of YOUR game.

> **YOUR ALPHAPRICING
> ARISES FROM YOUR
> ALPHAPASSION**

CHAPTER 3

IT IS NOT WHAT THEY WILL THINK IT IS

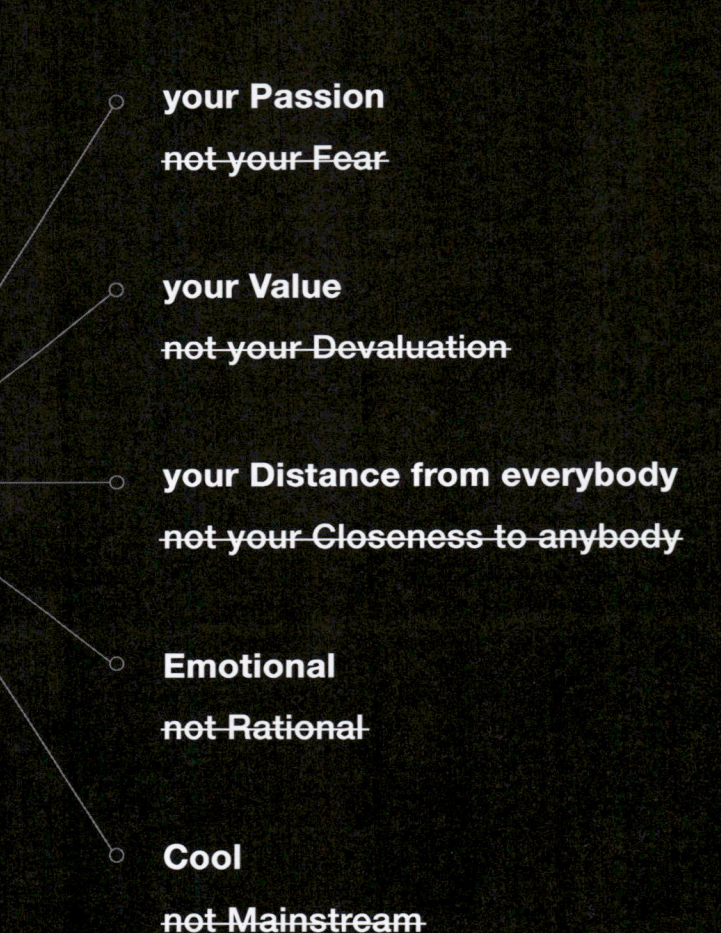

Price is

- your Passion
  ~~not your Fear~~

- your Value
  ~~not your Devaluation~~

- your Distance from everybody
  ~~not your Closeness to anybody~~

- Emotional
  ~~not Rational~~

- Cool
  ~~not Mainstream~~

CHAPTER 3

ALL HAIL TO THE
PRICENAUT

Do not overprice the basic brand so much, overprice the limited edition of the brand.

―――

Then, create an ultra-limited edition of the brand with a stratospheric price.

―――

The average price should always be as high as your high net worth customer would desire it to be.

―――

It's not about price, it's about emotions!

―――

As always, do not take advice from the so-called experts of the sector for they don't know anything at all.

CHAPTER 3

ME TOO? NO, LUCKY YOU!

Each brand has a USP.

Luxury Brands have ESP.

Your brand has **Your** ESP.

+

YOUR

Passion

Perfectionism

Craftsmanship

Uniqueness

**HOW SUITABLY
WILL YOU VALUE THESE?
I AM SURE THAT YOU WILL.**

CHAPTER 3

STEP 8

LUXURY COLLEGE STUDENT

CHAPTER 3

OFF
TO COLLEGE!

**We are taking things
to the next level.**

After thinking, learning and executing,
we are now launching the Brand.

We introduce our ESP and
achievement to the market.

Adolescence, foolish thoughts, fear
of imperfection, are all suddenly gone.

"I am capable of doing it".
This is your statement.

The Mysterious is there, along
with your passion to create and
your desire to launch.

**AS ALWAYS, THERE IS
SOMETHING MISSING**

CHAPTER 3

APPLYING KEY SECRET
SCARCITY

**It is not You who is scarce,
it is the Re-Invented You.**

———

Scarcity creates Value,
not vice versa.

Be it technical or authentic,
scarcity will always be at
the core of your Luxury Brand.

Aim to conquer the heart
of your consumer.
By conquering their heart,
you would create contradictory
emotions - so essential
in the Luxury Universe.

You shall not be within reach.

**LUXURY BRANDS
PLAY IT OUT OF REACH
TO KEEP YOU
WITHIN REACH**

CHAPTER 3

I AM
DISTANT

The more you create distance,
the more you are creating real value
to your Luxury Brand. This Key Secret
is by far the most important in terms
of sustaining your Brand to its Luxury
Level and extend it to future dynamics
as well.

Personally, I don't follow the ordinary
path and I am always looking for
other possibilities of creating
something completely different.

The ON and OFF message
is appealing to me.

And if you want to go out
and create a Luxury Brand,
it shall be to you, as well.

ON: It's not for me

OFF: It's SOMETIMES for me

**ON + OFF + ON + OFF +
ON + OFF. RELENTLESSLY**

CHAPTER 3

DISTANCE CONQUERS EMOTIONS

How to do it

Always & without exception

- Communicate price indirectly
- Communicate the Limited Editions
- Communicate the exact number of items you produce per day
- Communicate the names of the craftsmen that created this exquisite packaging
- Communicate Exclusive Events

- Name the celebrities that are customers
- Give your ultra premium edition to an influencer for a day and make a buzz about it
- Use PR to create word-of-mouth around your Brand
- Create synergies with a more established Luxury Brand in order to associate connections

CHAPTER 3

MIXED EMOTIONS
ADD MORE DISTANCE

Communicate that you are not offering ANY discounts

This helps attaining the symbolic power of a strong Luxury Brand.

As you can see, without creating Scarcity, you cannot do much. Scarcity shall always be built in advance, not after.

STRONG	+ OUT OF REACH	=	SCARCE
SCARCE	+ NO DISCOUNTS	=	VERY STRONG LUXURY BRAND
VERY STRONG LUXURY BRAND	+ FINE TUNING	=	SUCCESS

BUILD DISTANCE TO CREATE PROXIMITY

CHAPTER 3

LEAD
THROUGH SCARCITY WHEN NO ONE IS FOLLOWING

No matter if you are alone in your market and with an achievement in hand, you have to continuously build Scarcity associations.
You would never stop. NEVER.

Stopping will position your brand into the Premium Zone and - puff! - just like that, all the Value Added will be vanished!

Many entrepreneurs are making the same mistake over and over: they do the right things until one day they realize that their product isn't so hype anymore.

That's because the audience buying the brand is not so EXCLUSIVE anymore.

AND WHAT SHOULD YOU DO TO DRAW THE AUDIENCE'S ATTENTION AGAIN?

CHAPTER 3

RECREATE DISTANCE BY INCREASING THE PRICE!

Every time they sense that your brand is mass-oriented, you have to raise prices for it to become unreachable again.

Being too exclusive is a mess. You are becoming too Snobbish and no one would want to buy your Brand.

Being too mass, it's totally a mess. No one would appreciate your Brand. You shall not drastically change your price once you set it. For that, it is essential to make the right choice from the beginning.

> **THE MORE YOU FIND YOUR IN-BETWEEN, THE MORE SUCCESSFUL YOU WILL BE WITH YOUR VALUE ADDED**

CHAPTER 3

SCARCITY
24/7

\\

My name is Scarcity

———

I let go of my freedom
so to live inside your Brand.
I am the most precious of your rings,
the most valuable of your desires,
the most powerful of your emotions.

You shall be my guardian angel.
For years, months, days, passing
moments, you will be seeing me
for what I am: your treasure.
The most provocative challenge,
intriguing, thus, Rare.

**I AM THE MISTRESS
OF THE LUXURY UNIVERSE**

//

CHAPTER 3

STEP 9

LUXURY ADULT

CHAPTER 3

LOVE
YOUR
COPYCATS!

You are almost there

Your Luxury Baby has now become an Adult. Maturity kicks in and you are to face a new agenda.

First, you shall have to welcome the Copycats. Copycats are common ground for the Mysterious λ. To every unique idea, its imitator.

The more the counterfeit, the more successful your Luxury Brand is. You have achieved to create something that is sought after. Its value cannot be exactly measured at this stage (you have neither a major distribution network nor the geographical expansion), however Copycats would give you the first "little something": that of the excellent work you have done.

> **HAVE THEY COPIED YOUR MISSION? LOVE THE IDEA RATHER THAN HATE IT**

CHAPTER 3

EVERYTHING
THEY NEED, YOU GIVE THEM ASAP!

Service them like Kings & Queens

I am passionate about my work. I never let something out of control. NEVER. Please DO THE SAME. The key secret to succeed in any business is to love your work and be in love with your customers. Being in love means:

YOUR LUXURY BRAND CANNOT CHANGE TO FULFILL THEIR WISHES, BUT YOU SHOULD

- Treating your clients like Kings & Queens

- Offering them the best of your heart and soul because it will pay you off

- Understanding that not all of your customers are the same, some are very well-off, some aren't. Know the difference and behave accordingly

- Offering 24/7 online service for your e-shop? They will congratulate you many many times for that! You shall never stop giving them what they need, ask, feel or notice

CHAPTER 3

PR IS YOUR RIGHT HAND IF YOU ARE RIGHT HANDED

I have explained why hiring a PR pro on a monthly basis is such an essential aspect for a successful Luxury Brand.

This needs to be done BELOW THE LINE, UNDER THE RADAR of any given perception of your public. It works, it works really well, trust me. I have used this valuable tool many times with excellent results.

However, by using PR in Luxury it does not mean that you will be selling volumes of your brand. You will be building Luxury Brand Equity, instead.

Think of it as a continuous, brick by brick, building of Value. One PR action links to the next and that to the next etc. You should not care about sales during this process.

> **YOU ARE BUILDING A CONNECTION WITH YOUR CUSTOMER**

CHAPTER 3

SOCIAL MEDIA:
LET US MANIPULATE DESIRE.

A Valuable tool to create and recreate Demand

Daily + Weekly + Monthly + Yearly = Posts
aiming to promote your brand to your targeted affluent clientele

- The Creation of Desire = Posts presenting your Luxury brand with the symbolic value we have already explored (Snob but not too Snob, definitely elegant, superlative elements, association with other lifestyle symbols)

- The Recreation of Desire = Posts reminding of what your brand stands for (The Luxuriant Core, your ESP, Craftsmanship - but not your Luxury Pricing, of course!)

These two would generate global demand for the brand and visits to your ecommerce (which shall have to offer the best online retail experience available).

SOCIAL MEDIA IS YOUR EVERYDAY MANIPULATING BUFFER

CHAPTER 3

SALES ARE SLOW BUT BRAND VALUE IS
HUGE

Forget revenues

It's about a dream that evokes emotions

The most common mistake that EVERY newcomer in the Luxury Universe makes is that of huge revenues, becoming successful and rich within the first 4-5 years.

YOU WON'T MAKE THAT MISTAKE BECAUSE YOU ARE READING MY BOOK.

We shall have to understand that the Mysterious λ needs more time in order to be erotic and seductive. She desires to be comfortable enough before letting her charisma free. While this is happening, you shall be consistent, you shall have to take into account that Luxury Timeframe is more extensive than we think. You need to continue your Brick By Brick Luxury Mission.

THE MORE IS LUXURY, THE MORE IT TAKES TIME

CHAPTER 3

THOSE CONSISTENT WILL BE REWARDED

Learn everything about Consistency

When your Luxury Adult is slowly moving into the global market, you should not "push" trying to accelerate sales. Remember: you DON'T CARE about sales during this time. You care about building a powerful statement.

You want to be remembered as the creator of something exceptional.

Sales KILL exclusivity.
Sales DESTROY the dream.
Sales can DAMAGE the perception of the customer you are trying at this stage to attract.

You should not allow this to happen. You need to care about your Brand and protect it from any Low Value Harm (LVH). You will avoid by ANY MEANS this.

> **BE CONSISTENT TO YOUR LUXURY MISSION AND DO NOT LOOK AT YOUR WATCH**

CHAPTER 3

REMINDER.
IF YOU DIDN'T
FOLLOW THE STEPS
AS PROVIDED

DO NOT BOTHER READING ANY MORE OF THIS BOOK

CHAPTER 3

STEP 10

LUXURY ADULT
+
KICKING

CHAPTER 3

GO GLOBALLY BUT VALUE ORIENTED

This Step is when Luxury finally
shows her strength, the Profit Margin.
You will love it, I am sure, given that
you made it through all these Steps.

You are here (and there!), trying
to express your Luxury Statement
more and more.

The journey to Luxury is of No Time.
It always establishes itself as if it
was a river that stemmed from our
emotions. However, it needs to follow
strict steps with accuracy
and dedication.

Have you done it correctly?
Have you chosen value over sales?

CHAPTER 3

SLOW
BREAK-EVEN POINT. CONTINUE TO BUILD YOUR UNIQUE VISION WITH CONSISTENCY!

Break it slow, but Break it Even

This is where break even happens. And if you have done them all correctly, you WILL see it happen.

Assuming that all previous 9 Steps were followed, you will begin to:

- Expand your point of sales, as you will notice a small increase of demand
- Notice an increase of online sales, too
- Gain a significant number of loyal clients
- Notice that the publicity would come to you and not the other way round
- Notice other people appraise you for your achievement
- Witness more and more Copycats imitating your Luxury Brand

BUILDING VALUE AS A NON-STOP DANCE

What should you do at that Step? Continue your dedicated Mission within Luxury to reach your Breakeven Point

CHAPTER 3

DESIRABILITY,
IF PERFECTLY BUILT, NEVER REALLY FADES.

Customer + Luxury Brand = Very Tight Bond

Despite economic crises,
your customer WILL return.

I had many returning customers over the years, customers/early adopters who bought a few bottles ten years ago and then simply disappeared.

It's a typical phenomenon for Her: either a few of your customers are now a little bit distant from your brand (that doesn't mean that they are not appreciating it) or that their financial confidence is now low (for reasons you will never know).

Do not worry.
They will come back.

> **DESIRE ALWAYS RETURNS TO THE SCENE OF THE MYSTERIOUS λ.**

CHAPTER 3

HER
AS A
TRIBE.
BE A FAN, FIRST.

Your ESP is a Catalyst.

Many people would become fans because of it. Fans are useful, they create your first and most important core of believers.

They are followers of your vision and potential buyers of your brand. They would want to know about you and your brand. Do not fall into that trap. Her shall be always mysterious, aloof.

The approach could only be that of a friendly distance. When I gave away many of my cards to them, they lost their desire for my brand all at once.

To create, sustain and extend your Luxury Tribe, use On/Off techniques (Friendly and Distant) and be consistent to your unique vision. The more you promote your vision and passion, the more you will notice results to your fan base.

DIVE DEEP INTO YOUR TRIBE, FOR THEY ARE YOUR BEST WORD OF MOUTH

CHAPTER 3

SAY NO
TO LOW VALUED PLACEMENTS

Distribute rarity, not volumes

When you will be expanding your distribution network, you shall be asking yourself:

1/ **Is it the HIGH END retail point that I should be in?**

2/ **Is this communicating scarcity?**

Luxury NEEDS scarcity, even when you are expanding and selling.
It is about selling Scarcity once again.

DO NOT try to oversell at this Step. You WILL destroy all the Value you have already created.

> **WHEN YOU SELL SCARCITY, YOU BUY VALUE. WHEN YOU BUY VALUE, IT WILL RETURN AS BRAND EQUITY TO YOU**

CHAPTER 3

EXTEND
AFTER BREAK-EVEN

Break even?
Let's create another brand!

By the time you get to your Breakeven Point, you are becoming The Visionary You Have Proven To Be and then, you will create Your Next Luxury Brand. You shall be extending your series of products by being very cautious, though.

○ Not all of your passions are ideal for extension

○ You shall look for something that's a bit closer to your existing Luxury Brand

○ Never extend to a sector to which your company doesn't have expertise

○ Once you have chosen the extension, be the Perfectionist We Know You Are. Absorb anything about the subject and then go create

EXTEND LIKE A SPECIAL OPERATIONS MILITARY FORCE: SLOWLY BUT DECISIVELY, INTENSIVELY COLDBLOODED

CHAPTER 3

MEET
FOCUS
&
CONSISTENCY

○ **Focus**
is of essence in Luxury. In every Step, YOU SHALL HAVE to be very focused to your Luxury Mission. Never allow anyone and anything to get between your vision and your target to achieve it. By doing that, you shall know exactly what to do and how to react every time an issue arises.

○ **Consistency**
on the other hand, is THAT kind of trait in a character that GETS YOU THERE. Without being consistent, without doing the same actions every day that lead you closer to your Luxury vision, you cannot achieve anything at all. These two are my favorite personality assets

Try to cultivate them both in order to get to the final Step.

| **INTO THE IMPOSSIBLE**

CHAPTER 3

STEP 11

LUXURY ADULT
+
2X KICKING

CHAPTER 3

DON'T FEAR
THE REAPER

You are now entering
the last Step, you are
to reap what you sow.

Your business is starting to grow, slowly but steadily. You have developed an upscale distribution network worldwide.

You have also extended your series of Luxury Statements aka Luxury Brands.

But, as always happens in the Perfectionist's Mind…

THERE'S SOMETHING MISSING

CHAPTER 3

BENEFIT
FROM YOUR HIGH PROFIT MARGIN

Keep going, keep growing!

The benefits of creating and controlling Scarcity

- You will notice increasing revenues

- Profits will also get a huge increase, due to profit margin

- You will be compensated for many years of losses

- Your company will be evaluated way more than a mass-oriented company

- There will be a loyal clientele worldwide

Keep cool, but care

That's my favorite Thomas Pynchon quote. And one of my favorites in general

---

What does it mean for the Mysterious λ and your achievements?

It means to reap the benefits of your effort but NEVER EVER get to lose:

- ESP
- High price
- Scarcity
- Craftsmanship

> **YOU ARE DEFINED BY YOUR ACTIONS**

CHAPTER 3

ALWAYS STAY
SMART
AND DISTANT

Luxury Visionaries
AVOID

- Dreaming of huge factories with way too many working people, producing boring brands
- Relocating their premises to countries that are cheaper in terms of fixed and production costs, but would harm Brand Value
- Producing far too many volumes from one line of their products, therefore cannibalizing its Value
- Decreasing price as time goes by
- Promoting the brand on mass media publications (above the line), thus harm the Brand and turn it into a massclusive one

Luxury Visionaries
CONTINUE

- Envisioning the future and reinventing boring ideas into New Value Added Opportunities
- Inspiring their team to become the best in the world
- Absorbing anything that would lead into a new, impossible venture
- Going where it is happening, Always Out There In The Dirt
- Being inspired by indie and underground cultures in order to create really differentiated Value Added brands
- Inspiring others to follow that path

**BEING EXCLUSIVE =
MASTERING YOUR MISSION**

CHAPTER 3

> STEP 11

It is not about your Luxury Company's growth **only**

———

It is about your **Growth** as a Luxury Visionary

You are there and you shall continue to work to fine tune your Mission. Follow these 11 steps throughout time. Re-read them as many times as possible.

Then get to work.

| **AND, OF COURSE, SUCCEED**

APPENDIX

A FEW LAST WORDS

As an entrepreneur that has created a Luxury Brand, I have field-tested these strategies and I know that they work. I have also read a lot of academic books about the subject and, to tell you the truth, I was not exactly impressed.

Before I started following my Luxury Mission, I was into words, not actions. After that, I relentlessly read and applied, learned and executed, brain and action.

A CALL TO ACTION IS THE MOST IMPORTANT CALL YOU WILL EVER GET

APPENDIX

Before anything, this is a book about a Call To Action:

The action of creating extraordinary achievements that many people would love and be passionate with.

Luxury is not defined by books and brains, it is defined, first and most, by your unique way of defining your Mission, so unique that it creates Scarcity.

What is made of Passion, it is also made to Stand Out.

The motive behind any Transcendence of Μέτρον is, quite simply, to transcend yourself. To excel in something. To believe that you can achieve always more. And more. And More.

Have you ever wondered why trees have leaves? Do you see that leaf maneuvering on that tree? A tiny but significant action in the Tree of Life.

Evergreen dazed. Stand still. Do nothing. Hold your breath. Everything that's hiding, will start to reveal itself.

Then, all the extraordinariness of your Vision would come up and meet you. You shall embrace it and go with it.

You will always be trying to control a few, unique but contradictory emotions and turn them into desires.

You will succeed many times. You will miss other times. It doesn't matter as long as you go on.

After all, what is the Mysterious λ but a seductive woman, enigmatic and inexplicable, an emotional entity which would always escape us?

APPENDIX

ALWAYS

REMEMBER

APPENDIX

KEY SECRETS

| ① | ② | ③ | ④ |

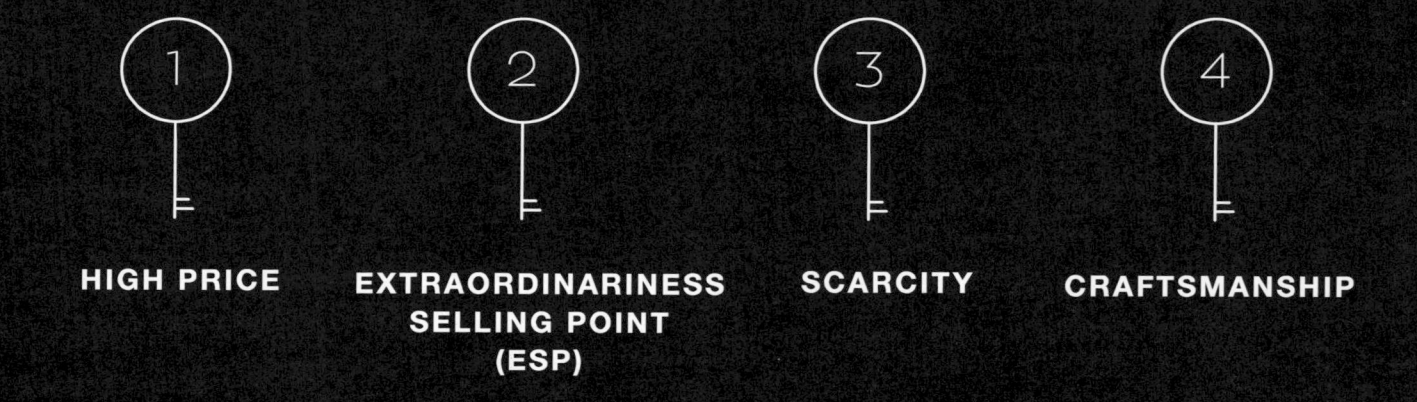

HIGH PRICE **EXTRAORDINARINESS SELLING POINT (ESP)** **SCARCITY** **CRAFTSMANSHIP**

APPENDIX

STEPS

01
02
03
04
05
06
07
08
09
10
11

LUXURY ADULT + 2X KICKING

LUXURY ADULT + KICKING

LUXURY ADULT

LUXURY COLLEGE STUDENT

LUXURY ADOLESCENT

LUXURY BABY

MOMENTUM BLAST

ESP APOCALYPSE

INNOVATION GAP

INNOVATOR MANIA

FAIL STUDENT

NOW
GO OUT
AND
SUCCEED

Printed by Amazon Italia Logistica S.r.l.
Torrazza Piemonte (TO), Italy